addresses

PETER PAUPER PRESS, INC.
White Plains, New York

PETER PAUPER PRESS
Fine Books and Gifts Since 1928

Our Company

In 1928, at the age of twenty-two, Peter Beilenson began printing books on a small press in the basement of his parents' home in Larchmont, New York. Peter—and later, his wife, Edna—sought to create fine books that sold at "prices even a pauper could afford."

Today, still family owned and operated, Peter Pauper Press continues to honor our founders' legacy—and our customers' expectations—of beauty, quality, and value.

Designed by Margaret Rubiano

Visit us at www.peterpauper.com

NAME

ADDRESS

HOME

MOBILE

WORK / FAX

EMAIL

NAME

ADDRESS

HOME

MOBILE

WORK / FAX

EMAIL

NAME

ADDRESS

HOME

MOBILE

WORK / FAX

EMAIL

NAME

ADDRESS

HOME

MOBILE

WORK / FAX

EMAIL

NAME

ADDRESS

HOME

MOBILE

WORK / FAX

EMAIL

NAME

ADDRESS

HOME

MOBILE

WORK / FAX

EMAIL

NAME

ADDRESS

HOME

MOBILE

WORK / FAX

EMAIL

NAME

ADDRESS

HOME

MOBILE

WORK / FAX

EMAIL

NAME

ADDRESS

HOME

MOBILE

WORK / FAX

EMAIL

NAME

ADDRESS

HOME

MOBILE

WORK / FAX

EMAIL

NAME

ADDRESS

HOME

MOBILE

WORK / FAX

EMAIL

NAME

ADDRESS

HOME

MOBILE

WORK / FAX

EMAIL

NAME

ADDRESS

HOME

MOBILE

WORK / FAX

EMAIL

NAME

ADDRESS

HOME

MOBILE

WORK / FAX

EMAIL

NAME

ADDRESS

HOME

MOBILE

WORK / FAX

EMAIL

NAME

ADDRESS

HOME

MOBILE

WORK / FAX

EMAIL

NAME

ADDRESS

HOME

MOBILE

WORK / FAX

EMAIL

NAME

ADDRESS

HOME

MOBILE

WORK / FAX

EMAIL

B

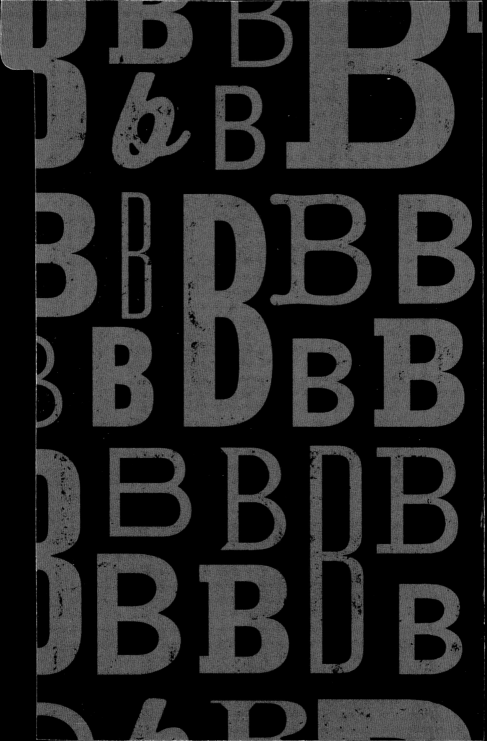

NAME

ADDRESS

HOME

MOBILE

WORK / FAX

EMAIL

NAME

ADDRESS

HOME

MOBILE

WORK / FAX

EMAIL

NAME

ADDRESS

HOME

MOBILE

WORK / FAX

EMAIL

NAME

ADDRESS

HOME

MOBILE

WORK / FAX

EMAIL

NAME

ADDRESS

HOME

MOBILE

WORK / FAX

EMAIL

NAME

ADDRESS

HOME

MOBILE

WORK / FAX

EMAIL

NAME

ADDRESS

HOME

MOBILE

WORK / FAX

EMAIL

NAME

ADDRESS

HOME

MOBILE

WORK / FAX

EMAIL

NAME

ADDRESS

HOME

MOBILE

WORK / FAX

EMAIL

NAME

ADDRESS

HOME

MOBILE

WORK / FAX

EMAIL

NAME

ADDRESS

HOME

MOBILE

WORK / FAX

EMAIL

NAME

ADDRESS

HOME

MOBILE

WORK / FAX

EMAIL

NAME

ADDRESS

HOME

MOBILE

WORK / FAX

EMAIL

NAME

ADDRESS

HOME

MOBILE

WORK / FAX

EMAIL

NAME

ADDRESS

HOME

MOBILE

WORK / FAX

EMAIL

NAME

ADDRESS

HOME

MOBILE

WORK / FAX

EMAIL

NAME

ADDRESS

HOME

MOBILE

WORK / FAX

EMAIL

NAME

ADDRESS

HOME

MOBILE

WORK / FAX

EMAIL

NAME

ADDRESS

HOME

MOBILE

WORK / FAX

EMAIL

NAME

ADDRESS

HOME

MOBILE

WORK / FAX

EMAIL

NAME

ADDRESS

HOME

MOBILE

WORK / FAX

EMAIL

NAME

ADDRESS

HOME

MOBILE

WORK / FAX

EMAIL

NAME

ADDRESS

HOME

MOBILE

WORK / FAX

EMAIL

NAME

ADDRESS

HOME

MOBILE

WORK / FAX

EMAIL

NAME

ADDRESS

HOME

MOBILE

WORK / FAX

EMAIL

NAME

ADDRESS

HOME

MOBILE

WORK / FAX

EMAIL

NAME

ADDRESS

HOME

MOBILE

WORK / FAX

EMAIL

NAME

ADDRESS

HOME

MOBILE

WORK / FAX

EMAIL

NAME

ADDRESS

HOME

MOBILE

WORK / FAX

EMAIL

NAME

ADDRESS

HOME

MOBILE

WORK / FAX

EMAIL

NAME

ADDRESS

HOME

MOBILE

WORK / FAX

EMAIL

NAME

ADDRESS

HOME

MOBILE

WORK / FAX

EMAIL

NAME

ADDRESS

HOME

MOBILE

WORK / FAX

EMAIL

NAME

ADDRESS

HOME

MOBILE

WORK / FAX

EMAIL

NAME

ADDRESS

HOME

MOBILE

WORK / FAX

EMAIL

NAME

ADDRESS

HOME

MOBILE

WORK / FAX

EMAIL

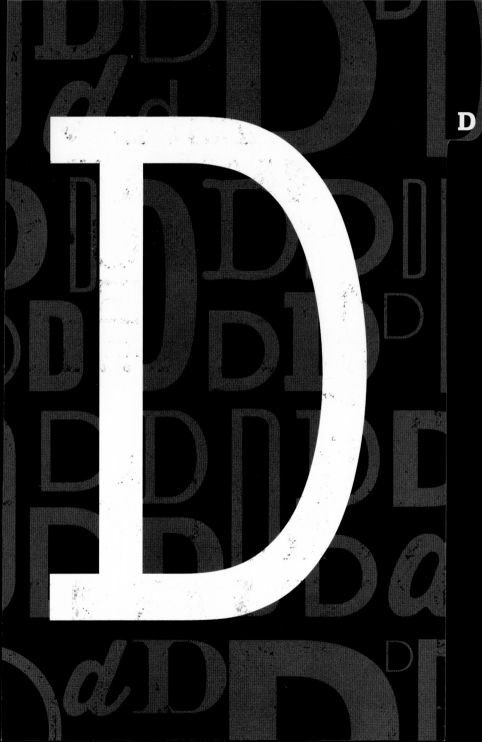

D

NAME

ADDRESS

HOME

MOBILE

WORK / FAX

EMAIL

NAME

ADDRESS

HOME

MOBILE

WORK / FAX

EMAIL

NAME

ADDRESS

HOME

MOBILE

WORK / FAX

EMAIL

NAME

ADDRESS

HOME

MOBILE

WORK / FAX

EMAIL

NAME

ADDRESS

HOME

MOBILE

WORK / FAX

EMAIL

NAME

ADDRESS

HOME

MOBILE

WORK / FAX

EMAIL

NAME

ADDRESS

HOME

MOBILE

WORK / FAX

EMAIL

NAME

ADDRESS

HOME

MOBILE

WORK / FAX

EMAIL

NAME

ADDRESS

HOME

MOBILE

WORK / FAX

EMAIL

NAME

ADDRESS

HOME

MOBILE

WORK / FAX

EMAIL

NAME

ADDRESS

HOME

MOBILE

WORK / FAX

EMAIL

NAME

ADDRESS

HOME

MOBILE

WORK / FAX

EMAIL

NAME

ADDRESS

HOME

MOBILE

WORK / FAX

EMAIL

NAME

ADDRESS

HOME

MOBILE

WORK / FAX

EMAIL

NAME

ADDRESS

HOME

MOBILE

WORK / FAX

EMAIL

NAME

ADDRESS

HOME

MOBILE

WORK / FAX

EMAIL

NAME

ADDRESS

HOME

MOBILE

WORK / FAX

EMAIL

NAME

ADDRESS

HOME

MOBILE

WORK / FAX

EMAIL

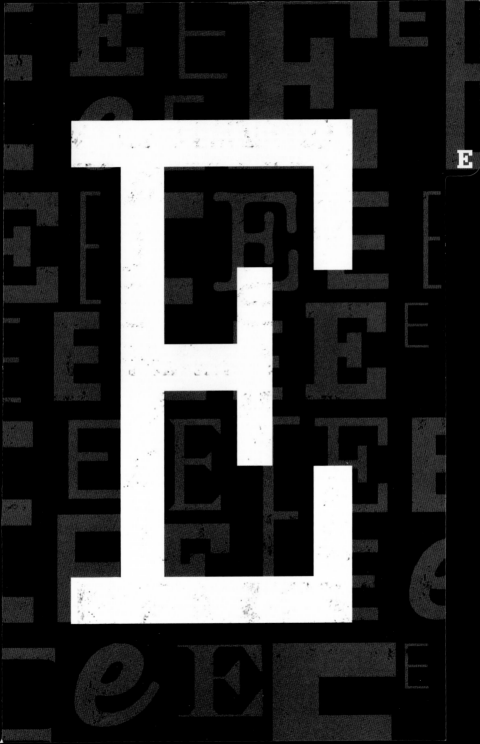

E

NAME

ADDRESS

HOME

MOBILE

WORK / FAX

EMAIL

NAME

ADDRESS

HOME

MOBILE

WORK / FAX

EMAIL

NAME

ADDRESS

HOME

MOBILE

WORK / FAX

EMAIL

NAME

ADDRESS

HOME

MOBILE

WORK / FAX

EMAIL

NAME

ADDRESS

HOME

MOBILE

WORK / FAX

EMAIL

NAME

ADDRESS

HOME

MOBILE

WORK / FAX

EMAIL

NAME

ADDRESS

HOME

MOBILE

WORK / FAX

EMAIL

NAME

ADDRESS

HOME

MOBILE

WORK / FAX

EMAIL

NAME

ADDRESS

HOME

MOBILE

WORK / FAX

EMAIL

NAME

ADDRESS

HOME

MOBILE

WORK / FAX

EMAIL

NAME

ADDRESS

HOME

MOBILE

WORK / FAX

EMAIL

NAME

ADDRESS

HOME

MOBILE

WORK / FAX

EMAIL

NAME

ADDRESS

HOME

MOBILE

WORK / FAX

EMAIL

NAME

ADDRESS

HOME

MOBILE

WORK / FAX

EMAIL

NAME

ADDRESS

HOME

MOBILE

WORK / FAX

EMAIL

NAME

ADDRESS

HOME

MOBILE

WORK / FAX

EMAIL

NAME

ADDRESS

HOME

MOBILE

WORK / FAX

EMAIL

NAME

ADDRESS

HOME

MOBILE

WORK / FAX

EMAIL

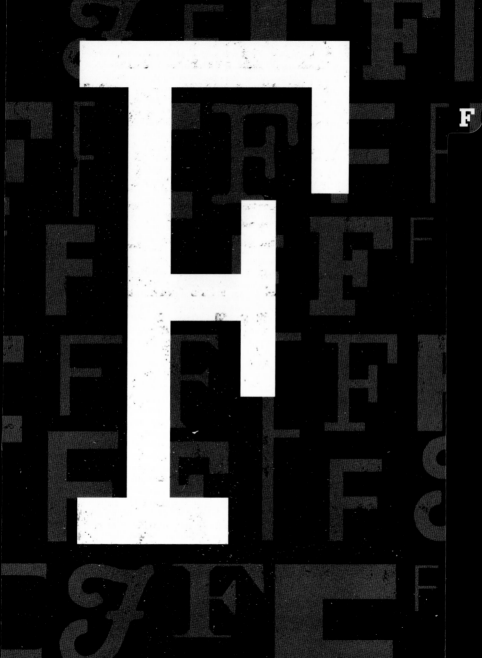

NAME

ADDRESS

HOME

MOBILE

WORK / FAX

EMAIL

NAME

ADDRESS

HOME

MOBILE

WORK / FAX

EMAIL

NAME

ADDRESS

HOME

MOBILE

WORK / FAX

EMAIL

NAME

ADDRESS

HOME

MOBILE

WORK / FAX

EMAIL

NAME

ADDRESS

HOME

MOBILE

WORK / FAX

EMAIL

NAME

ADDRESS

HOME

MOBILE

WORK / FAX

EMAIL

NAME

ADDRESS

HOME

MOBILE

WORK / FAX

EMAIL

NAME

ADDRESS

HOME

MOBILE

WORK / FAX

EMAIL

NAME

ADDRESS

HOME

MOBILE

WORK / FAX

EMAIL

NAME

ADDRESS

HOME

MOBILE

WORK / FAX

EMAIL

NAME

ADDRESS

HOME

MOBILE

WORK / FAX

EMAIL

NAME

ADDRESS

HOME

MOBILE

WORK / FAX

EMAIL

NAME

ADDRESS

HOME

MOBILE

WORK / FAX

EMAIL

NAME

ADDRESS

HOME

MOBILE

WORK / FAX

EMAIL

NAME

ADDRESS

HOME

MOBILE

WORK / FAX

EMAIL

NAME

ADDRESS

HOME

MOBILE

WORK / FAX

EMAIL

NAME

ADDRESS

HOME

MOBILE

WORK / FAX

EMAIL

NAME

ADDRESS

HOME

MOBILE

WORK / FAX

EMAIL

G

NAME

ADDRESS

HOME

MOBILE

WORK / FAX

EMAIL

NAME

ADDRESS

HOME

MOBILE

WORK / FAX

EMAIL

NAME

ADDRESS

HOME

MOBILE

WORK / FAX

EMAIL

NAME

ADDRESS

HOME

MOBILE

WORK / FAX

EMAIL

NAME

ADDRESS

HOME

MOBILE

WORK / FAX

EMAIL

NAME

ADDRESS

HOME

MOBILE

WORK / FAX

EMAIL

NAME

ADDRESS

HOME

MOBILE

WORK / FAX

EMAIL

NAME

ADDRESS

HOME

MOBILE

WORK / FAX

EMAIL

NAME

ADDRESS

HOME

MOBILE

WORK / FAX

EMAIL

NAME

ADDRESS

HOME

MOBILE

WORK / FAX

EMAIL

NAME

ADDRESS

HOME

MOBILE

WORK / FAX

EMAIL

NAME

ADDRESS

HOME

MOBILE

WORK / FAX

EMAIL

NAME

ADDRESS

HOME

MOBILE

WORK / FAX

EMAIL

NAME

ADDRESS

HOME

MOBILE

WORK / FAX

EMAIL

NAME

ADDRESS

HOME

MOBILE

WORK / FAX

EMAIL

NAME

ADDRESS

HOME

MOBILE

WORK / FAX

EMAIL

NAME

ADDRESS

HOME

MOBILE

WORK / FAX

EMAIL

NAME

ADDRESS

HOME

MOBILE

WORK / FAX

EMAIL

NAME

ADDRESS

HOME

MOBILE

WORK / FAX

EMAIL

NAME

ADDRESS

HOME

MOBILE

WORK / FAX

EMAIL

NAME

ADDRESS

HOME

MOBILE

WORK / FAX

EMAIL

NAME

ADDRESS

HOME

MOBILE

WORK / FAX

EMAIL

NAME

ADDRESS

HOME

MOBILE

WORK / FAX

EMAIL

NAME

ADDRESS

HOME

MOBILE

WORK / FAX

EMAIL

NAME

ADDRESS

HOME

MOBILE

WORK / FAX

EMAIL

NAME

ADDRESS

HOME

MOBILE

WORK / FAX

EMAIL

NAME

ADDRESS

HOME

MOBILE

WORK / FAX

EMAIL

NAME

ADDRESS

HOME

MOBILE

WORK / FAX

EMAIL

NAME

ADDRESS

HOME

MOBILE

WORK / FAX

EMAIL

NAME

ADDRESS

HOME

MOBILE

WORK / FAX

EMAIL

NAME

ADDRESS

HOME

MOBILE

WORK / FAX

EMAIL

NAME

ADDRESS

HOME

MOBILE

WORK / FAX

EMAIL

NAME

ADDRESS

HOME

MOBILE

WORK / FAX

EMAIL

NAME

ADDRESS

HOME

MOBILE

WORK / FAX

EMAIL

NAME

ADDRESS

HOME

MOBILE

WORK / FAX

EMAIL

NAME

ADDRESS

HOME

MOBILE

WORK / FAX

EMAIL

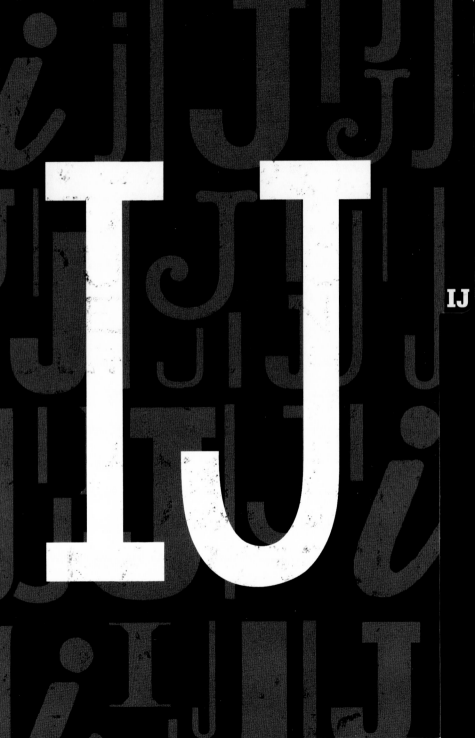

IJ

NAME

ADDRESS

HOME

MOBILE

WORK / FAX

EMAIL

NAME

ADDRESS

HOME

MOBILE

WORK / FAX

EMAIL

NAME

ADDRESS

HOME

MOBILE

WORK / FAX

EMAIL

NAME

ADDRESS

HOME

MOBILE

WORK / FAX

EMAIL

NAME

ADDRESS

HOME

MOBILE

WORK / FAX

EMAIL

NAME

ADDRESS

HOME

MOBILE

WORK / FAX

EMAIL

NAME

ADDRESS

HOME

MOBILE

WORK / FAX

EMAIL

NAME

ADDRESS

HOME

MOBILE

WORK / FAX

EMAIL

NAME

ADDRESS

HOME

MOBILE

WORK / FAX

EMAIL

NAME

ADDRESS

HOME

MOBILE

WORK / FAX

EMAIL

NAME

ADDRESS

HOME

MOBILE

WORK / FAX

EMAIL

NAME

ADDRESS

HOME

MOBILE

WORK / FAX

EMAIL

NAME

ADDRESS

HOME

MOBILE

WORK / FAX

E-MAIL

NAME

ADDRESS

HOME

MOBILE

WORK / FAX

E-MAIL

NAME

ADDRESS

HOME

MOBILE

WORK / FAX

E-MAIL

NAME

ADDRESS

HOME

MOBILE

WORK / FAX

EMAIL

NAME

ADDRESS

HOME

MOBILE

WORK / FAX

EMAIL

NAME

ADDRESS

HOME

MOBILE

WORK / FAX

EMAIL

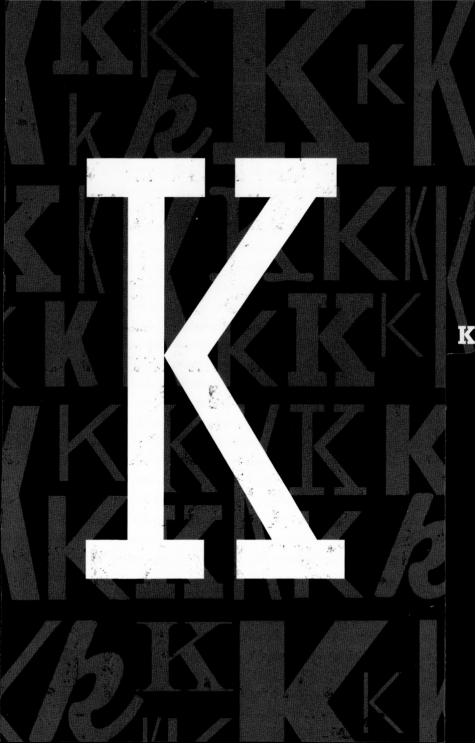

NAME

ADDRESS

HOME

MOBILE

WORK / FAX

MAIL

NAME

ADDRESS

HOME

MOBILE

WORK / FAX

MAIL

NAME

ADDRESS

HOME

MOBILE

WORK / FAX

MAIL

NAME

ADDRESS

HOME

MOBILE

WORK / FAX

EMAIL

NAME

ADDRESS

HOME

MOBILE

WORK / FAX

EMAIL

NAME

ADDRESS

HOME

MOBILE

WORK / FAX

EMAIL

NAME

ADDRESS

HOME

MOBILE

WORK / FAX

EMAIL

NAME

ADDRESS

HOME

MOBILE

WORK / FAX

EMAIL

NAME

ADDRESS

HOME

MOBILE

WORK / FAX

EMAIL

NAME

ADDRESS

HOME

MOBILE

WORK / FAX

EMAIL

NAME

ADDRESS

HOME

MOBILE

WORK / FAX

EMAIL

NAME

ADDRESS

HOME

MOBILE

WORK / FAX

EMAIL

NAME

ADDRESS

HOME

MOBILE

WORK / FAX

E-MAIL

NAME

ADDRESS

HOME

MOBILE

WORK / FAX

E-MAIL

NAME

ADDRESS

HOME

MOBILE

WORK / FAX

E-MAIL

NAME

ADDRESS

HOME

MOBILE

WORK / FAX

EMAIL

NAME

ADDRESS

HOME

MOBILE

WORK / FAX

EMAIL

NAME

ADDRESS

HOME

MOBILE

WORK / FAX

EMAIL

NAME

ADDRESS

HOME

MOBILE

WORK / FAX

EMAIL

NAME

ADDRESS

HOME

MOBILE

WORK / FAX

EMAIL

NAME

ADDRESS

HOME

MOBILE

WORK / FAX

EMAIL

NAME

ADDRESS

HOME

MOBILE

WORK / FAX

EMAIL

NAME

ADDRESS

HOME

MOBILE

WORK / FAX

EMAIL

NAME

ADDRESS

HOME

MOBILE

WORK / FAX

EMAIL

NAME

ADDRESS

HOME

MOBILE

WORK / FAX

EMAIL

NAME

ADDRESS

HOME

MOBILE

WORK / FAX

EMAIL

NAME

ADDRESS

HOME

MOBILE

WORK / FAX

EMAIL

NAME

ADDRESS

HOME

MOBILE

WORK / FAX

EMAIL

NAME

ADDRESS

HOME

MOBILE

WORK / FAX

EMAIL

NAME

ADDRESS

HOME

MOBILE

WORK / FAX

EMAIL

NAME

ADDRESS

HOME

MOBILE

WORK / FAX

EMAIL

NAME

ADDRESS

HOME

MOBILE

WORK / FAX

EMAIL

NAME

ADDRESS

HOME

MOBILE

WORK / FAX

EMAIL

NAME

ADDRESS

HOME

MOBILE

WORK / FAX

EMAIL

NAME

ADDRESS

HOME

MOBILE

WORK / FAX

EMAIL

NAME

ADDRESS

HOME

MOBILE

WORK / FAX

EMAIL

NAME

ADDRESS

HOME

MOBILE

WORK / FAX

E-MAIL

NAME

ADDRESS

HOME

MOBILE

WORK / FAX

E-MAIL

NAME

ADDRESS

HOME

MOBILE

WORK / FAX

E-MAIL

NAME

ADDRESS

HOME

MOBILE

WORK / FAX

EMAIL

NAME

ADDRESS

HOME

MOBILE

WORK / FAX

EMAIL

NAME

ADDRESS

HOME

MOBILE

WORK / FAX

EMAIL

NAME

ADDRESS

HOME

MOBILE

WORK / FAX

EMAIL

NAME

ADDRESS

HOME

MOBILE

WORK / FAX

EMAIL

NAME

ADDRESS

HOME

MOBILE

WORK / FAX

EMAIL

NAME

ADDRESS

HOME

MOBILE

WORK / FAX

EMAIL

NAME

ADDRESS

HOME

MOBILE

WORK / FAX

EMAIL

NAME

ADDRESS

HOME

MOBILE

WORK / FAX

EMAIL

NAME

ADDRESS

HOME

MOBILE

WORK / FAX

MAIL

NAME

ADDRESS

HOME

MOBILE

WORK / FAX

MAIL

NAME

ADDRESS

HOME

MOBILE

WORK / FAX

MAIL

NAME

ADDRESS

HOME

MOBILE

WORK / FAX

EMAIL

NAME

ADDRESS

HOME

MOBILE

WORK / FAX

EMAIL

NAME

ADDRESS

HOME

MOBILE

WORK / FAX

EMAIL

NAME

ADDRESS

HOME

MOBILE

WORK / FAX

EMAIL

NAME

ADDRESS

HOME

MOBILE

WORK / FAX

EMAIL

NAME

ADDRESS

HOME

MOBILE

WORK / FAX

EMAIL

NAME

ADDRESS

HOME

MOBILE

WORK / FAX

EMAIL

NAME

ADDRESS

HOME

MOBILE

WORK / FAX

EMAIL

NAME

ADDRESS

HOME

MOBILE

WORK / FAX

EMAIL

NAME

ADDRESS

HOME

MOBILE

WORK / FAX

EMAIL

NAME

ADDRESS

HOME

MOBILE

WORK / FAX

EMAIL

NAME

ADDRESS

HOME

MOBILE

WORK / FAX

EMAIL

NAME

ADDRESS

HOME

MOBILE

WORK / FAX

EMAIL

NAME

ADDRESS

HOME

MOBILE

WORK / FAX

EMAIL

NAME

ADDRESS

HOME

MOBILE

WORK / FAX

EMAIL

NAME

ADDRESS

HOME

MOBILE

WORK / FAX

EMAIL

NAME

ADDRESS

HOME

MOBILE

WORK / FAX

EMAIL

NAME

ADDRESS

HOME

MOBILE

WORK / FAX

EMAIL

NAME

ADDRESS

HOME

MOBILE

WORK / FAX

EMAIL

NAME

ADDRESS

HOME

MOBILE

WORK / FAX

EMAIL

NAME

ADDRESS

HOME

MOBILE

WORK / FAX

EMAIL

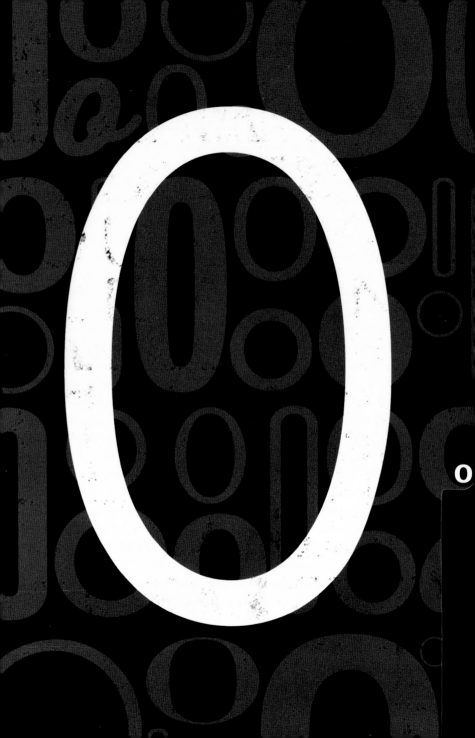

o

NAME

ADDRESS

HOME

MOBILE

WORK / FAX

EMAIL

NAME

ADDRESS

HOME

MOBILE

WORK / FAX

EMAIL

NAME

ADDRESS

HOME

MOBILE

WORK / FAX

EMAIL

NAME

ADDRESS

HOME

MOBILE

WORK / FAX

EMAIL

NAME

ADDRESS

HOME

MOBILE

WORK / FAX

EMAIL

NAME

ADDRESS

HOME

MOBILE

WORK / FAX

EMAIL

NAME

ADDRESS

HOME

MOBILE

WORK / FAX

MAIL

NAME

ADDRESS

HOME

MOBILE

WORK / FAX

MAIL

NAME

ADDRESS

HOME

MOBILE

WORK / FAX

MAIL

NAME

ADDRESS

HOME

MOBILE

WORK / FAX

EMAIL

NAME

ADDRESS

HOME

MOBILE

WORK / FAX

EMAIL

NAME

ADDRESS

HOME

MOBILE

WORK / FAX

EMAIL

NAME

ADDRESS

HOME

MOBILE

WORK / FAX

EMAIL

NAME

ADDRESS

HOME

MOBILE

WORK / FAX

EMAIL

NAME

ADDRESS

HOME

MOBILE

WORK / FAX

EMAIL

NAME

ADDRESS

HOME

MOBILE

WORK / FAX

EMAIL

NAME

ADDRESS

HOME

MOBILE

WORK / FAX

EMAIL

NAME

ADDRESS

HOME

MOBILE

WORK / FAX

EMAIL

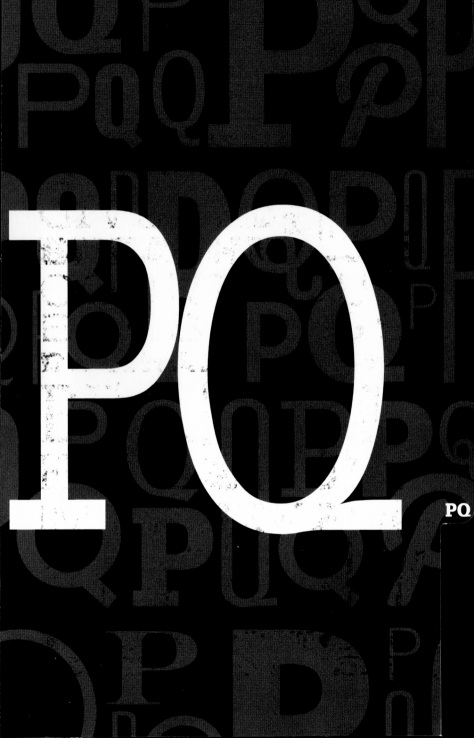

PQ

NAME

ADDRESS

NAME

MOBILE

WORK / FAX

MAIL

NAME

ADDRESS

NAME

MOBILE

WORK / FAX

MAIL

NAME

ADDRESS

NAME

MOBILE

WORK / FAX

MAIL

NAME

ADDRESS

HOME

MOBILE

WORK / FAX

EMAIL

NAME

ADDRESS

HOME

MOBILE

WORK / FAX

EMAIL

NAME

ADDRESS

HOME

MOBILE

WORK / FAX

EMAIL

ME

DRESS

ME

BILE

RK / FAX

AIL

ME

DRESS

ME

BILE

RK / FAX

AIL

ME

DRESS

ME

BILE

RK / FAX

AIL

NAME

ADDRESS

HOME

MOBILE

WORK / FAX

EMAIL

NAME

ADDRESS

HOME

MOBILE

WORK / FAX

EMAIL

NAME

ADDRESS

HOME

MOBILE

WORK / FAX

EMAIL

NAME

ADDRESS

NAME

MOBILE

WORK / FAX

EMAIL

NAME

ADDRESS

NAME

MOBILE

WORK / FAX

EMAIL

NAME

ADDRESS

NAME

MOBILE

WORK / FAX

EMAIL

NAME

ADDRESS

HOME

MOBILE

WORK / FAX

EMAIL

NAME

ADDRESS

HOME

MOBILE

WORK / FAX

EMAIL

NAME

ADDRESS

HOME

MOBILE

WORK / FAX

EMAIL

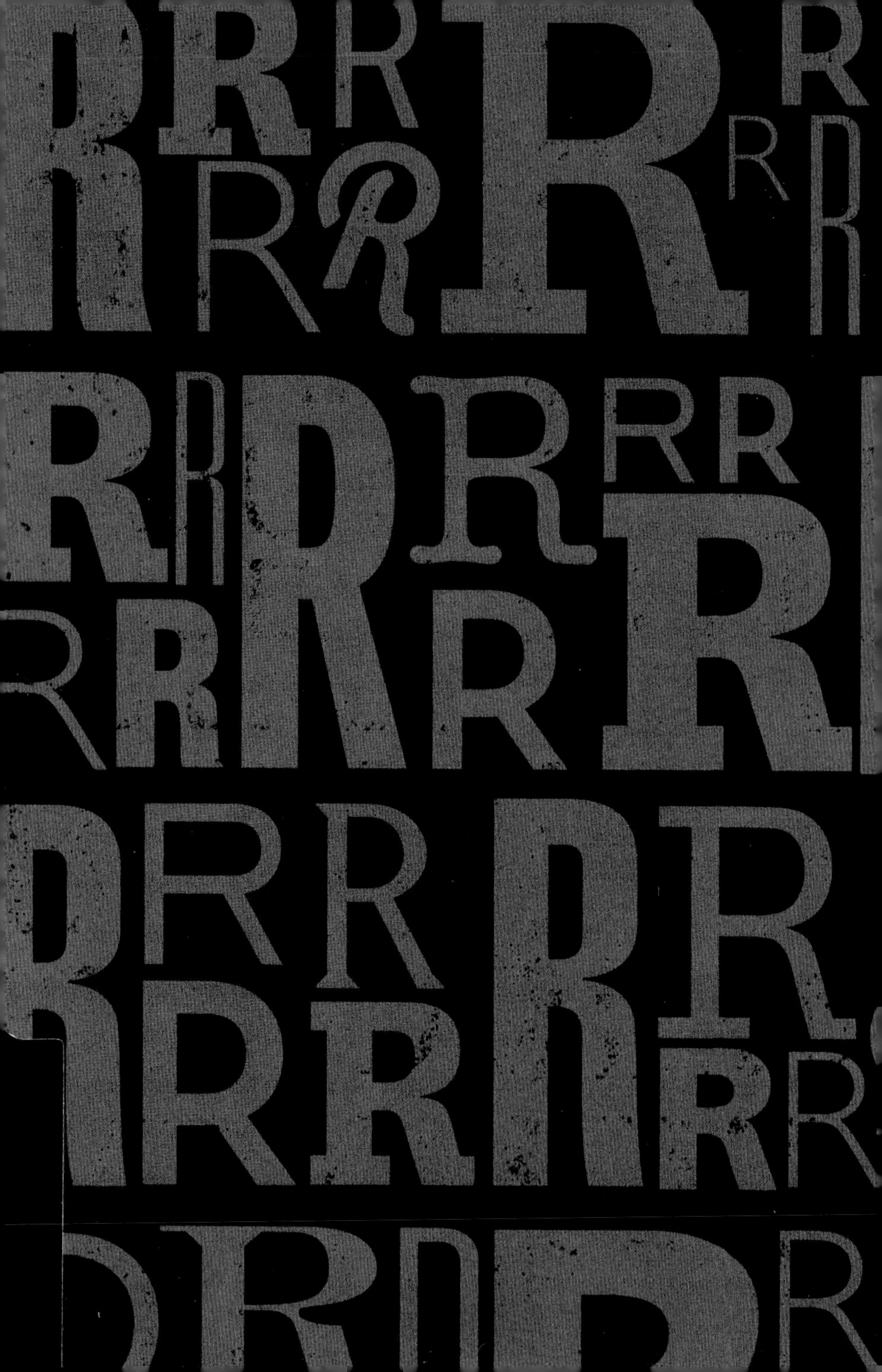

NAME

ADDRESS

HOME

MOBILE

WORK / FAX

EMAIL

NAME

ADDRESS

HOME

MOBILE

WORK / FAX

EMAIL

NAME

ADDRESS

HOME

MOBILE

WORK / FAX

EMAIL

NAME

ADDRESS

HOME

MOBILE

WORK / FAX

EMAIL

NAME

ADDRESS

HOME

MOBILE

WORK / FAX

EMAIL

NAME

ADDRESS

HOME

MOBILE

WORK / FAX

EMAIL

NAME

ADDRESS

HOME

MOBILE

WORK / FAX

EMAIL

NAME

ADDRESS

HOME

MOBILE

WORK / FAX

EMAIL

NAME

ADDRESS

HOME

MOBILE

WORK / FAX

EMAIL

NAME

ADDRESS

HOME

MOBILE

WORK / FAX

EMAIL

NAME

ADDRESS

HOME

MOBILE

WORK / FAX

EMAIL

NAME

ADDRESS

HOME

MOBILE

WORK / FAX

EMAIL

NAME

ADDRESS

HOME

MOBILE

WORK / FAX

EMAIL

NAME

ADDRESS

HOME

MOBILE

WORK / FAX

EMAIL

NAME

ADDRESS

HOME

MOBILE

WORK / FAX

EMAIL

NAME

ADDRESS

HOME

MOBILE

WORK / FAX

EMAIL

NAME

ADDRESS

HOME

MOBILE

WORK / FAX

EMAIL

NAME

ADDRESS

HOME

MOBILE

WORK / FAX

EMAIL

S

ME

DRESS

ME

OBILE

ORK / FAX

MAIL

NAME

DDRESS

OME

OBILE

ORK / FAX

MAIL

AME

DDRESS

OME

OBILE

WORK / FAX

MAIL

NAME

ADDRESS

HOME

MOBILE

WORK / FAX

EMAIL

NAME

ADDRESS

HOME

MOBILE

WORK / FAX

EMAIL

NAME

ADDRESS

HOME

MOBILE

WORK / FAX

EMAIL

NAME

ADDRESS

NAME

MOBILE

WORK / FAX

MAIL

NAME

ADDRESS

NAME

MOBILE

WORK / FAX

MAIL

NAME

ADDRESS

NAME

MOBILE

WORK / FAX

MAIL

NAME

ADDRESS

HOME

MOBILE

WORK / FAX

EMAIL

NAME

ADDRESS

HOME

MOBILE

WORK / FAX

EMAIL

NAME

ADDRESS

HOME

MOBILE

WORK / FAX

EMAIL

NAME

ADDRESS

HOME

MOBILE

WORK / FAX

MAIL

NAME

ADDRESS

HOME

MOBILE

WORK / FAX

MAIL

NAME

ADDRESS

HOME

MOBILE

WORK / FAX

MAIL

NAME

ADDRESS

HOME

MOBILE

WORK / FAX

EMAIL

NAME

ADDRESS

HOME

MOBILE

WORK / FAX

EMAIL

NAME

ADDRESS

HOME

MOBILE

WORK / FAX

EMAIL

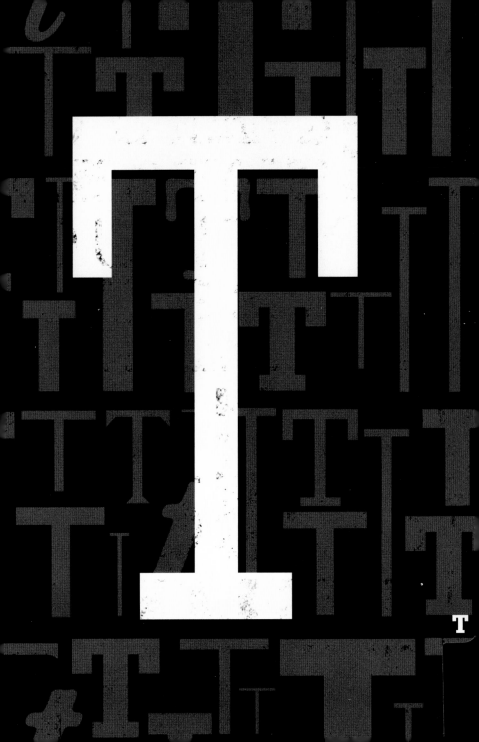

ME

DRESS

ME

BILE

RK / FAX

AIL

ME

DRESS

ME

BILE

RK / FAX

AIL

ME

DRESS

ME

BILE

RK / FAX

AIL

NAME

ADDRESS

HOME

MOBILE

WORK / FAX

EMAIL

NAME

ADDRESS

HOME

MOBILE

WORK / FAX

EMAIL

NAME

ADDRESS

HOME

MOBILE

WORK / FAX

EMAIL

NAME

ADDRESS

NAME

MOBILE

WORK / FAX

MAIL

NAME

ADDRESS

NAME

MOBILE

WORK / FAX

MAIL

NAME

ADDRESS

NAME

MOBILE

WORK / FAX

MAIL

NAME

ADDRESS

HOME

MOBILE

WORK / FAX

EMAIL

NAME

ADDRESS

HOME

MOBILE

WORK / FAX

EMAIL

NAME

ADDRESS

HOME

MOBILE

WORK / FAX

EMAIL

NAME

ADDRESS

NAME

MOBILE

WORK / FAX

EMAIL

NAME

ADDRESS

NAME

MOBILE

WORK / FAX

EMAIL

NAME

ADDRESS

NAME

MOBILE

WORK / FAX

EMAIL

NAME

ADDRESS

HOME

MOBILE

WORK / FAX

EMAIL

NAME

ADDRESS

HOME

MOBILE

WORK / FAX

EMAIL

NAME

ADDRESS

HOME

MOBILE

WORK / FAX

EMAIL

NAME

ADDRESS

HOME

MOBILE

WORK / FAX

EMAIL

NAME

ADDRESS

HOME

MOBILE

WORK / FAX

EMAIL

NAME

ADDRESS

HOME

MOBILE

WORK / FAX

EMAIL

NAME

ADDRESS

HOME

MOBILE

WORK / FAX

EMAIL

NAME

ADDRESS

HOME

MOBILE

WORK / FAX

EMAIL

NAME

ADDRESS

HOME

MOBILE

WORK / FAX

EMAIL

ME

DRESS

ME

BILE

RK / FAX

AIL

ME

DRESS

ME

BILE

RK / FAX

AIL

ME

DRESS

ME

BILE

RK / FAX

AIL

NAME

ADDRESS

HOME

MOBILE

WORK / FAX

EMAIL

NAME

ADDRESS

HOME

MOBILE

WORK / FAX

EMAIL

NAME

ADDRESS

HOME

MOBILE

WORK / FAX

EMAIL

NAME

ADDRESS

NAME

MOBILE

WORK / FAX

MAIL

NAME

ADDRESS

NAME

MOBILE

WORK / FAX

MAIL

NAME

ADDRESS

NAME

MOBILE

WORK / FAX

MAIL

NAME

ADDRESS

HOME

MOBILE

WORK / FAX

EMAIL

NAME

ADDRESS

HOME

MOBILE

WORK / FAX

EMAIL

NAME

ADDRESS

HOME

MOBILE

WORK / FAX

EMAIL

NAME

ADDRESS

NAME

MOBILE

WORK / FAX

EMAIL

NAME

ADDRESS

NAME

MOBILE

WORK / FAX

EMAIL

NAME

ADDRESS

NAME

MOBILE

WORK / FAX

EMAIL

NAME

ADDRESS

HOME

MOBILE

WORK / FAX

EMAIL

NAME

ADDRESS

HOME

MOBILE

WORK / FAX

EMAIL

NAME

ADDRESS

HOME

MOBILE

WORK / FAX

EMAIL

ME

DRESS

ME

BILE

RK / FAX

AIL

ME

DRESS

ME

BILE

RK / FAX

AIL

ME

DRESS

ME

BILE

RK / FAX

AIL

NAME

ADDRESS

HOME

MOBILE

WORK / FAX

EMAIL

NAME

ADDRESS

HOME

MOBILE

WORK / FAX

EMAIL

NAME

ADDRESS

HOME

MOBILE

WORK / FAX

EMAIL

ME

DRESS

ME

BILE

RK / FAX

AIL

ME

DRESS

ME

BILE

RK / FAX

AIL

ME

DRESS

ME

BILE

RK / FAX

AIL

NAME

ADDRESS

HOME

MOBILE

WORK / FAX

EMAIL

NAME

ADDRESS

HOME

MOBILE

WORK / FAX

EMAIL

NAME

ADDRESS

HOME

MOBILE

WORK / FAX

EMAIL

ME

DRESS

ME

BILE

RK / FAX

AIL

ME

DRESS

ME

BILE

RK / FAX

AIL

ME

DRESS

ME

BILE

RK / FAX

AIL

NAME

ADDRESS

HOME

MOBILE

WORK / FAX

EMAIL

NAME

ADDRESS

HOME

MOBILE

WORK / FAX

EMAIL

NAME

ADDRESS

HOME

MOBILE

WORK / FAX

EMAIL

XYZ

NAME

ADDRESS

HOME

MOBILE

WORK / FAX

EMAIL

NAME

ADDRESS

HOME

MOBILE

WORK / FAX

EMAIL

NAME

ADDRESS

HOME

MOBILE

WORK / FAX

EMAIL

NAME

ADDRESS

HOME

MOBILE

WORK / FAX

EMAIL

NAME

ADDRESS

HOME

MOBILE

WORK / FAX

EMAIL

NAME

ADDRESS

HOME

MOBILE

WORK / FAX

EMAIL

NAME

ADDRESS

HOME

MOBILE

WORK / FAX

EMAIL

NAME

ADDRESS

HOME

MOBILE

WORK / FAX

EMAIL

NAME

ADDRESS

HOME

MOBILE

WORK / FAX

EMAIL

NAME

ADDRESS

HOME

MOBILE

WORK / FAX

EMAIL

NAME

ADDRESS

HOME

MOBILE

WORK / FAX

EMAIL

NAME

ADDRESS

HOME

MOBILE

WORK / FAX

EMAIL

NAME

ADDRESS

HOME

MOBILE

WORK / FAX

EMAIL

NAME

ADDRESS

HOME

MOBILE

WORK / FAX

EMAIL

NAME

ADDRESS

HOME

MOBILE

WORK / FAX

EMAIL

NAME

ADDRESS

HOME

MOBILE

WORK / FAX

EMAIL

NAME

ADDRESS

HOME

MOBILE

WORK / FAX

EMAIL

NAME

ADDRESS

HOME

MOBILE

WORK / FAX

EMAIL

NAME

ADDRESS

HOME

MOBILE

WORK / FAX

EMAIL

NAME

ADDRESS

HOME

MOBILE

WORK / FAX

EMAIL

NAME

ADDRESS

HOME

MOBILE

WORK / FAX

EMAIL

NAME

ADDRESS

HOME

MOBILE

WORK / FAX

EMAIL

NAME

ADDRESS

HOME

MOBILE

WORK / FAX

EMAIL

NAME

ADDRESS

HOME

MOBILE

WORK / FAX

EMAIL

NAME

ADDRESS

HOME

MOBILE

WORK / FAX

EMAIL

NAME

ADDRESS

HOME

MOBILE

WORK / FAX

EMAIL

NAME

ADDRESS

HOME

MOBILE

WORK / FAX

EMAIL

International Dialing Codes

To make an international call, dial the **Out Code** of the country you're calling from, then the **In Code** of the country you're calling.

Country	Dial In	Dial Out	Country	Dial In	Dial Out
AFGHANISTAN	93	00	ISRAEL	972	00
ARGENTINA	54	00	ITALY	39	00
AUSTRALIA	61	0011	JAPAN	81	010
AUSTRIA	43	00	KENYA	254	000
BELGIUM	32	00	KOREA (SOUTH)	82	001
BELIZE	501	00	MEXICO	52	00
BRAZIL	55	0014	NETHERLANDS	31	00
CANADA	1	011	NEW ZEALAND	64	00
CHINA	86	00	NICARAGUA	505	00
COSTA RICA	506	00	NORWAY	47	00
CZECH REP.	420	00	PANAMA	507	00
DENMARK	45	00	PHILIPPINES	63	00
ECUADOR	593	00	POLAND	48	00
EGYPT	20	00	PORTUGAL	351	00
EL SALVADOR	503	00	RUSSIA	7	8~10
FRANCE	33	00	SINGAPORE	65	001
GERMANY	49	00	SOUTH AFRICA	27	00
GREECE	30	00	SPAIN	34	00
GUATEMALA	502	00	SWEDEN	46	00
HONDURAS	504	00	SWITZERLAND	41	00
HONG KONG	852	001	TAIWAN	886	002
ICELAND	354	00	THAILAND	66	001
INDIA	91	00	TURKEY	90	00
INDONESIA	62	001	UK	44	00
IRAQ	964	00	USA	1	011
IRELAND*	353	00			

Except Northern Ireland, which is part of the United Kingdom

For any country not listed here, visit *www.countrycallingcodes.com*